W9-CBG-142

Tsunamis

ANN O. SQUIRE

Children's Press®
An Imprint of Scholastic Inc.

Content Consultant
William Barnart, PhD
Assistant Professor
Department of Earth and Environmental Sciences
University of Iowa
Iowa City, Iowa

Library of Congress Cataloging-in-Publication Data
Squire, Ann O., author.
Tsunamis / by Ann O. Squire.
 pages cm. — (A true book)
 Summary: "Learn all about the violent waves known as tsunamis, from how they are formed to how they can affect people around the world"— Provided by publisher.
 Includes bibliographical references and index.
 ISBN 978-0-531-22298-0 (library binding : alk. paper) — ISBN 978-0-531-22514-1 (pbk. : alk. paper)
 1. Tsunamis—Juvenile literature. 2. Waves—Juvenile literature. 3. Tsunami damage—Juvenile literature. I. Title. II. Series: True book.
 GC221.5.S735 2016
 551.46'37—dc23   2015020020

© 2016 Scholastic Inc.
All rights reserved. Published in 2016 by Children's Press, an imprint of Scholastic Inc.
Printed in China 62
SCHOLASTIC, CHILDREN'S PRESS, A TRUE BOOK™, and associated logos are trademarks and/or registered trademarks of Scholastic Inc.
1 2 3 4 5 6 7 8 9 10 R 25 24 23 22 21 20 19 18 17 16

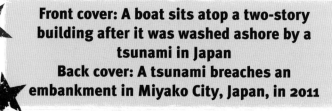

**Front cover: A boat sits atop a two-story building after it was washed ashore by a tsunami in Japan
Back cover: A tsunami breaches an embankment in Miyako City, Japan, in 2011**

Find the Truth!

Everything you are about to read is true *except* for one of the sentences on this page.

Which one is **TRUE**?

T or F Most tsunamis are the result of earthquakes beneath the ocean floor.

T or F All underwater earthquakes cause tsunamis.

Find the answers in this book.

Contents

THE BIG TRUTH!

An Important Geography Lesson

3 Tsunamis Around the World

Movements of the earth
can cause a tsunami.

4

A powerful tsunami wave tosses cars as if they were toys.

4 Preparing for the Worst

What tools do experts use to forecast
and prepare for tsunamis? **37**

The Krakatau tsunami affected ships as far away as South Africa.

People enjoy a beautiful sunset on the coast of Sumatra.

CHAPTER 1

What on Earth?

It was a beautiful morning on the Indonesian island of Sumatra the day after Christmas in 2004. Tourists and locals were relaxing on the beach, splashing in the warm waters of the Indian Ocean. To the people enjoying the sun and sand, it didn't seem as though anything could spoil this perfect day. However, just 150 miles (241 kilometers) away, beneath the seafloor, something big was happening. It would change the lives of everyone on the beach that day.

 People often have little or no warning before a tsunami strikes.

Earthquake

Nineteen miles (30.6 km) below the surface of the ocean, the earth moved. The powerful earthquake ripped along a fault 600 miles (1,000 km) long. People in Sumatra felt the shaking most intensely, but it could also be felt for hundreds of miles in every direction. Scientists later classified the quake as a **magnitude** 9.0. It was the world's third-largest earthquake since 1900.

The center of the 2004 underwater earthquake was located very close to Sumatra.

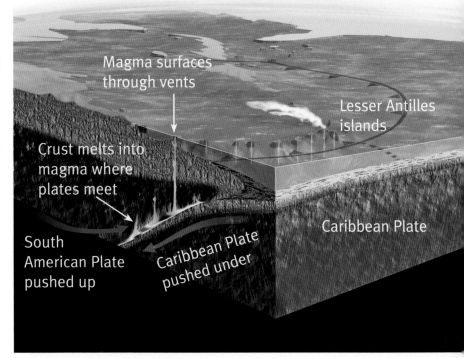

The South American and Caribbean plates meet and grind against each other beneath the Caribbean Sea.

Magma surfaces through vents

Lesser Antilles islands

Crust melts into magma where plates meet

Caribbean Plate

South American Plate pushed up

Caribbean Plate pushed under

Caribbean Plate

After the Earthquake

The shaking went on for several long minutes. When it finally stopped, everything was quiet. It seemed as though the worst was over. But far out to sea, something more devastating was forming. The quake had moved a portion of the ocean floor, pushing it sideways and upward by about 30 feet (10 meters). Millions of gallons of ocean water were abruptly shoved upward with it.

A swell in ocean water does not make a very big difference in the vast open water.

This underwater push created a pulse of energy that traveled in all directions from the fault **rupture**. This pulse was a **tsunami**. In the middle of the ocean, the tsunami did not look like much. It appeared to be a large swell, just a foot or two higher than the surrounding water. To a sailor on the huge open ocean, the swell would have been hardly noticeable. For people on the shore, it was going to be a different story.

Killer Tsunami

The tsunami raced toward shore at the speed of a jet airplane. About 20 minutes after the earthquake had set off the tsunami, people on Sumatra's beaches began to feel its effects. The ocean began to recede quickly. It was as if the tide was going out much faster and farther than normal. It left fish stranded and boats and coral reefs high and dry.

As the ocean water recedes, swimmers might suddenly find themselves standing in the sand.

A few minutes later, the water surged back in. This was the first of the tsunami waves, or bores, and it was more powerful than anyone had imagined. In some places, the tsunami was 50 feet (15 m) high. As the water rushed inland, it carried people, cars, boats, and buildings with it. Then the water rushed out again, sweeping many people out to sea. Many more bores would arrive over the next several hours.

People run from an oncoming wave during the 2004 tsunami in Sumatra.

The 2004 tsunami flattened and washed away buildings across a wide area.

By the end of the day, hundreds of thousands of people were injured, dead, or missing in Indonesia alone. The tsunami also caused damage in several other countries, including some as far away as South Africa, 5,000 miles (8,047 km) from the earthquake's **epicenter**. Scientists estimated that the tsunami had carried an energy equal to 23,000 atomic bombs.

Like an earthquake, a volcanic eruption can suddenly unleash a wave of powerful energy.

What Causes a Tsunami?

Many events can create a tsunami. An underwater landslide, a volcanic eruption, and a meteor impact are some examples. The most common cause is an earthquake beneath the ocean floor. Underwater earthquakes are responsible for three-quarters of all tsunamis. How exactly does an earthquake happen, and how can it create a tsunami? To understand, it helps to know a little bit about Earth's outer layers.

A volcanic eruption can sometimes trigger a tsunami.

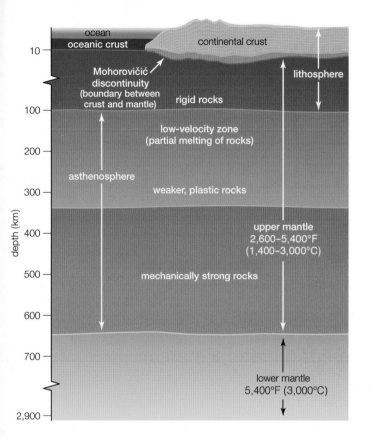

depth (km)

10	ocean
	oceanic crust	continental crust
	Mohorovičić discontinuity (boundary between crust and mantle)	lithosphere
100	rigid rocks
	low-velocity zone (partial melting of rocks)
200	
	asthenosphere	weaker, plastic rocks
300	
400	upper mantle 2,600–5,400°F (1,400–3,000°C)
500	mechanically strong rocks
600	
700	lower mantle 5,400°F (3,000°C)
2,900	

The temperature is extremely high in the planet's deeper layers.

Tectonic Plates

Our planet's hard outer shell is called the lithosphere. It includes Earth's outermost layer, called the crust, and the highest, solid part of the mantle below it. The lithosphere is broken up into large chunks called tectonic plates. Beneath the plates is the asthenosphere. The asthenosphere is also solid rock, but it is hotter and softer than the lithosphere. The tectonic plates move above the softer asthenosphere, shifting and sliding past one another.

Earth's tectonic plates are constantly shifting. This movement is very slow—about as fast as your fingernails grow. The plates may slide past one another, as they do at the San Andreas Fault in California. They can also move farther apart or closer together. The two plates off Sumatra's coast that caused the 2004 earthquake and tsunami are moving closer together. One plate (the Indian Plate) is gradually sliding underneath the other (the Burma Plate).

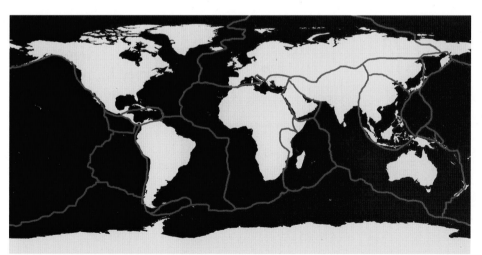

Earthquakes are most common along the places where Earth's tectonic plates meet (shown by red lines).

How an Earthquake Happens

Although tectonic plates are made of rock, they are somewhat flexible. As the Indian Plate slides under the Burma Plate, both bend a tiny bit. The more they press against each other, the more each plate is pushed out of shape. The stress on both plates increases. Eventually, the pressure becomes too great and the plates spring back to their original shape. As they do, they release tremendous amounts of energy, resulting in an earthquake.

The Himalaya Mountains were formed by movement of the Indian Plate.

Severe earthquakes can lower nearby coastlines, allowing tsunamis to travel farther inland.

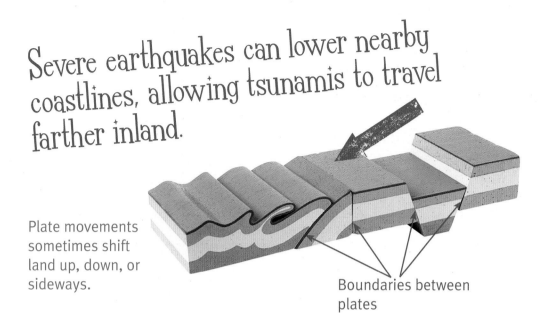

Plate movements sometimes shift land up, down, or sideways.

Boundaries between plates

From Earthquake to Tsunami

Some strong underwater earthquakes shift the seafloor up or down. This gives the ocean water above a powerful push, creating a tsunami. In the deep ocean, the tsunami looks fairly small. This changes as it moves into shallow water near the coast. The bottom of the tsunami slows down as it travels among sand, rocks, and organisms on the seafloor, but the top of the tsunami still moves fast. The water piles up into a giant wall of water.

To cause a tsunami, an earthquake must move the seafloor a significant amount either up or down. Earthquakes below 7.0 out of 10 on the earthquake magnitude scale don't displace, or move, enough water to create a tsunami. Also, if the seafloor shifts sideways instead of up or down, a tsunami will not occur. In addition, the earthquake's epicenter must be near Earth's surface. Deeper quakes usually do not change the shape of the seafloor.

This diagram illustrates how waves rush toward shore as the water recedes from the coast following an underwater earthquake.

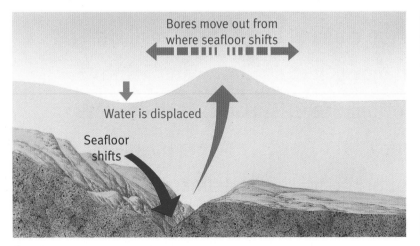

Bores move out from where seafloor shifts

Water is displaced

Seafloor shifts

Reaching Shore

A tsunami often consists of a series of bores called a wave train. The first bore may not be as strong as those that come later. Sometimes the first part of the tsunami to reach land is a trough, or low space between bores. If this happens, the water rushes out from the shore much farther and faster than normal. A surge of water soon follows as the first bore in the wave train arrives.

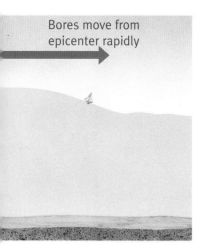

Bores move from epicenter rapidly

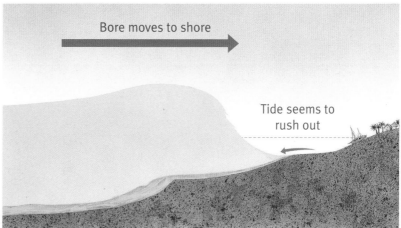

Bore moves to shore

Tide seems to rush out

The amount of damage a tsunami does is closely related to the **topography** of the seafloor and land. Obstacles such as coral reefs between the open ocean and the land can lessen a tsunami's strength as it approaches shore. Hills and mountains stop the water from traveling as far as it would on flat land. In addition, if high ground is nearby and easy for people to reach, many lives may be saved.

A coral reef can help weaken tsunami waves before they reach the shore.

Harbor Wave

The word *tsunami* comes from two Japanese words: *tsu*, meaning "harbor," and *nami*, meaning "wave." Experts think that fishermen in Japan originally coined the term "harbor wave." These people returned from a day at sea to find that a giant wave had destroyed their villages. Because a tsunami bore is barely noticeable in the open ocean, the fishers likely believed that the tsunamis arose only when they entered the harbor.

An Important Geography Lesson

In 2004, 10-year-old Tilly Smith and her family left cold and rainy England to spend Christmas on the beach in Phuket, Thailand. They were enjoying the water on the morning of December 26 when Tilly noticed that the ocean looked strange. The tide was rushing out much too quickly. The water bubbled. Boats on the horizon bobbed violently up and down.

A few weeks earlier, Tilly's geography class had studied earthquakes and tsunamis. Tilly recognized the signs that a tsunami might be on the way. She alerted her parents, who told the staff at their hotel. Everyone left the beach and ran for higher ground. The tsunami rushed in a few minutes later, reaching heights of up to 50 feet (15 m). Thanks to Tilly, no one in the area was killed or seriously injured. Officials estimate that Tilly's actions saved at least 100 lives.

A boat sails near Anak Krakatau volcano during a 2011 eruption.

CHAPTER 3

Tsunamis Around the World

In terms of lives lost, the 2004 Indian Ocean tsunami was the worst in history. But over the years, destructive tsunamis have occurred in many places around the world. In Indonesia, a volcanic island named Krakatau erupted in 1883. The eruption took place over several days and destroyed two-thirds of the island. Besides releasing a rain of burning ash, the Krakatau eruption created several strong tsunamis.

A new volcano is forming where Krakatau once stood.

Many Fatalities

The eruption of Krakatau was one of the most powerful volcanic eruptions in history. The sound of the explosion was so loud that people heard it from thousands of miles away. Historians estimate more than 36,000 people lost their lives. But despite the volcano's destructive power, most of the victims were killed not by the eruption, but by the tsunamis that came afterward.

The eruption of Krakatau unleashed a huge cloud of dust and ash into the air.

The waves that followed Krakatau's eruption were tremendously damaging.

Landslide

The tsunamis from Krakatau's explosion weren't formed the way tsunamis are formed by earthquakes. Instead, they arose as huge sections of the island, along with hot gases and rock fragments from the volcano, slid into the sea. This displaced millions of gallons of water. Making matters worse, many of the surrounding islands were low-lying, without large hills or mountains to slow the tide. This allowed the tsunamis to be especially destructive. Some islands were wiped out completely.

The 1755 Lisbon earthquake caused entire buildings to crumble.

The Great Lisbon Earthquake . . .

On November 1, 1755, the Catholic holiday of All Saints' Day, most residents of Lisbon, Portugal, were in church. At 9:40 AM, a strong earthquake hit the city. Several large cathedrals collapsed, killing everyone inside. The city was reduced to rubble within minutes. Soon, fires broke out. Afraid for their lives, many people ran down to Lisbon's waterfront, where they thought they would be safe from the fires and collapsing buildings.

. . . and Tsunami

The earthquake's epicenter was 120 miles (193 km) offshore. Its force had generated a tsunami. About 40 minutes after the quake, huge bores rushed in. They destroyed much of the harbor and downtown area. The tsunami affected not only Lisbon but also other coastal cities in Portugal, Spain, and Morocco. More than 70,000 people lost their lives.

Around 85 percent of Lisbon was destroyed by the earthquake and tsunami of 1755.

Residents of a fishing port in Japan watch as tsunami walls are constructed to help protect the town from future disasters.

Disaster in Japan

Earthquakes and tsunamis are common in Japan. Only 50 miles (80.5 km) off the eastern shore, one tectonic plate slides beneath another. The country has earthquake and tsunami early warning systems. Many coastal towns also have seawalls for protection from tsunamis. Though these precautions helped before, they were not enough on March 11, 2011. That day, a 9.0 magnitude earthquake struck northeastern Japan. It pushed part of the seafloor up by roughly 30 feet (10 m).

In many coastal towns, water surged over the seawalls, destroying buildings and sweeping people out to sea. The tsunami was felt in Hawaii, Mexico, and the west coast of the continent of North America. Waves even reached Antarctica, more than 8,000 miles (12,875 km) from the epicenter. The force of the waves caused a chunk of ice the size of New York City's Manhattan Island to break off of an ice shelf. And another problem was also occurring.

The city of Miyako, Japan, was one of the locations hit by the 2011 tsunami.

Meltdown

A number of nuclear facilities are located along Japan's eastern coast. When the quake hit, power at these facilities automatically shut down. With backup **generators**, the plants could keep their nuclear reactors safely cooled. But when the tsunami arrived, it flooded the generators at one facility, Fukushima Daiichi. The plant was left without power. Temperatures in its reactors rose quickly. Military helicopters scooped up seawater and poured it on the plant to try to cool it.

Damage to the Fukushima power plant during the 2011 disaster created another danger for the people of Japan.

Huge crowds of people were evacuated to makeshift shelters in the wake of the 2011 tsunami.

Unfortunately, that didn't work. The reactors overheated, and their cores melted down. This caused fires, explosions, and a release of dangerous levels of **radiation** in the surrounding area. More than 100,000 people were **evacuated** from their homes when high radiation levels made it unsafe to stay. Years later, officials are still working to make the area safe, but the process is slow. By 2015, many people had still not returned home.

Signs are posted in many coastal areas to inform people what they should do if a tsunami occurs.

CHAPTER 4

Preparing for the Worst

Nothing can stop a tsunami once it starts. However, early warning can reduce destruction and, most importantly, save lives. Some parts of the world have good tsunami warning systems, while others do not. One reason the 2004 tsunami was so destructive is that no warning system was in place in the Indian Ocean at that time. The tsunami caught many people by surprise and, as a result, more than 230,000 people died.

In flat coastal areas, it may be impossible to escape a tsunami.

Scientists at the Pacific Tsunami Warning Center rely on measurements and advanced computer software to help them predict natural disasters.

The Limits of Prediction

Around the Pacific Ocean, where most tsunamis occur, warning systems have been in place for many years. Using data from **seismometers**, officials issue an advisory or warning when they detect a strong ocean earthquake. However, most earthquakes don't result in tsunamis, and seismometers alone give incomplete information about whether a tsunami will occur. As a result, these warnings are often false alarms.

A Fast Forecast

Scientists work toward better ways to forecast tsunamis, especially for areas near an earthquake epicenter, where tsunamis would quickly follow. In combination with seismometers, experts often use ocean buoys and tide stations that sense tiny changes in water level. These tools are designed to detect both the earthquake and any significant change in tide or water level. This allows officials to issue more accurate tsunami advisories and warnings, even within minutes of a quake.

Buoys can provide a lot of information about what is happening below the surface of the ocean.

Underwater Sensors

For places farther from an earthquake epicenter, officials have more time to gather data. The Deep-Ocean Assessment and Reporting of Tsunamis (DART) system helps with this through the use of **tsunameters**. These sensors on the ocean floor pick up the slightest change in water pressure. They can detect a change in sea level of less than 0.5 inches (1.3 centimeters). The sensors send signals to buoys on the surface, which relay the information via satellite to warning centers.

Timeline of Major Tsunamis

1883

Indonesia's volcano Krakatau erupts, causing far-reaching tsunamis.

November 1, 1755

A major earthquake and tsunami hit Portugal, Spain, and Morocco.

Keeping People Safe

Communities must also plan how to protect people in the event of a disaster. Some researchers study the frequency, size, and location of past tsunamis. They do this by looking at layers of deposits—mud, plants, animals, and other materials a tsunami leaves behind—in an area. This information helps them design seawalls and other protective measures. When a tsunami is detected, computer simulations of a tsunami's path help experts plan the best evacuation routes.

March 11, 2011

A tsunami in northeastern Japan sets off a nuclear disaster.

December 26, 2004

One of the largest tsunamis in history hits coastlines across the Indian Ocean.

Residents of Chile follow signs to safe locations during a 2014 tsunami.

A good warning system can provide people with several minutes to several hours to escape a tsunami. If you live near a coastline, you need to know what to do, and you need to act fast. Learn the early warning signs of a tsunami (see page 43). Many locations have sirens that go off when a tsunami is approaching. Find out whether your community has evacuation routes or shelters. Plan with your family what to do if an emergency arises. These activities could save your life.

Surviving a Tsunami

How do you survive a tsunami? Here are some tips.

Be aware of an earthquake: If you feel an earthquake, head to higher ground.

Watch for a quickly receding tide: A tide that goes out unusually far or fast can be a signal that a tsunami is on the way.

Keep clear of rivers and streams: Tsunamis can surge up rivers and streams. Stay away from them even if you think you're a safe distance from the coast.

Watch for a wave train: There may be more than one bore, and the first bore in the series may not be the largest. Even if the first bore has passed, don't assume you are out of danger.

Don't delay: Head to higher ground as fast as you can. Tsunamis reach shore very quickly. You may not have time to escape if you wait until you see an approaching bore. ★

Highest tsunami bore ever recorded: 1,719 ft. (524 m)

Average speed at which tsunami bores can move across the ocean: 500 mph (805 kph)

Number of deaths that resulted from the 2004 Indian Ocean tsunami: More than 230,000

Number of people affected by the 2004 Indian Ocean tsunami: More than 5 million

Total lives lost in the Krakatau eruption and tsunami in 1883: More than 36,000

Average number of tsunamis that occur somewhere in the world each year: 2

Average number of years between major, destructive, ocean-wide tsunamis: 15

Did you find the truth?

(T) Most tsunamis are the result of earthquakes beneath the ocean floor.

(F) All underwater earthquakes cause tsunamis.

Resources

Books

Buck, Pearl S. *The Big Wave*. New York: HarperCollins, 1986.

Tarshis, Lauren. *I Survived the Japanese Tsunami, 2011*. New York: Scholastic, 2013.

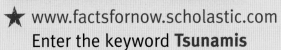

Visit this Scholastic Web site for more information on tsunamis:
www.factsfornow.scholastic.com
Enter the keyword **Tsunamis**

Important Words

epicenter (EP-i-sen-tur) — the area directly above where an earthquake occurs

evacuated (i-VAK-yoo-ate-id) — moved away from an area because it is dangerous there

generators (JEN-uh-ray-turz) — machines that produce electricity

magnitude (MAG-ni-tood) — the size or importance of something

radiation (ray-dee-AY-shuhn) — atomic particles that are sent out from a substance whose nuclei break down, giving off energy

rupture (RUHP-chur) — a break or opening

seismometers (size-MAH-mih-turz) — instruments that detect earthquakes and measure their power

topography (tuh-PAH-gruh-fee) — the physical features of an area, including hills, valleys, mountains, plains, and rivers

tsunameters (tsoo-NAH-mih-turz) —instruments used for the early detection, measurement, and real-time reporting of tsunamis in the open ocean

tsunami (tsoo-NAH-mee) — a very large, destructive surge of water caused by an underwater disturbance

Index

Page numbers in **bold** indicate illustrations.

About the Author

Ann O. Squire is a psychologist and an animal behaviorist. Before becoming a writer, she studied the behavior of rats, tropical fish in the Caribbean, and electric fish from central Africa. Her favorite part of being a writer is the chance to learn as much as she can about all sorts of topics. In addition to the *Extreme Earth* books, Dr. Squire has written about many different animals, from lemmings to leopards and cicadas to cheetahs. She lives in Long Island City, New York.